This book is dedicated to Gilda O'Neill who for many years was a great friend of Newham Bookshop. Gilda, an Eastender, listened to locals' stories and then wrote about them and encouraged others to do the same. The Gilda Street Trust continues Gilda's work and supported this publication.

Ada Varley, reader   p.32

4   *Vivian Archer, bookseller*   *p.37*

Kay Zahmoul, reader   p.31   5

6   *John Newman, bookseller*   *p.57*

Jools Walker, writer   p.54

8   *Vaseem Khan, writer*   *p.82*

Irenosen Okojie, writer   p.49

10   *Suresh Singh, writer* *p.76*

Carel Buxton, reader   p.81

Luan Goldie, writer *p.64*

Pete May, writer   p.42   13

14   *Barbara Mackenzie, reader   p.61*

Karima Turay-Davis, reader   *p.74*   15

16   *Safiyah Saeed, reader   p.80*

A Bookshop for All:
Conversations with Newham's
Readers and Writers

Edited by Rosa Schling
Foreword by Michael Rosen
Photographs by Fatimah Zahmoul
Oral history recorded by Rosa Schling
and Tania Aubeelack

First published by On the Record, 2022

On the Record
33 Birdsmouth Court
London
N15 4FW

⸨OnTheRecord

British Library Cataloguing in Publication Data
A CIP catalogue record for this book is available from
the British Library

ISBN 978-0-9927393-3-1

This book was designed, typeset and made into pages
in Adobe InDesign by Guglielmo Rossi, Bandiera

The text was set in the typeface GT Alpina regular and italic
The book was printed and bound by Gomer Press Ltd

This publication was published with financial support from
the Gilda Steet Trust

on-the-record.org.uk

A
Bookshop
for All

Thank you to:

all the people interviewed for Writing and Reading Newham for generously sharing their memories, experiences, and time with us

the Gilda Street Trust who funded this work in the memory of author, and friend of the bookshop, Gilda O'Neill

everyone at Newham Bookshop, especially Vivian Archer

Tania Aubeelack, for all your work on the interviews, learning resources and planning this book

Fatimah Zahmoul, for the photography

Michael Rosen, for the foreword

Guglielmo Rossi, for design and typesetting

Stefan Dickers and his colleagues at Bishopsgate Institute, for giving the archive a safe home

Susan Hutton, for the transcription

Richard Whittell, for proof reading, editing and so much more.

Foreword
Michael Rosen

Newham Bookshop is much more than a bookshop. It's a philosophy.

Again and again I've seen at first hand how this is a bookshop that does all that it can to make a bridge between authors and readers. All the people who work there, headed of course by Vivian Archer, bring writers and readers together. This could be just a cosy matter of sticking to a coterie of people who might find their way to a bookshop anyway, but with this bookshop it involves a potent mix of a wide range of writers and a wide range of audiences. But what does 'wide' mean? It means paying close attention to diversity and disadvantage (not the same thing, I hasten to add!).

Diversity: the bookshop has always had a responsibility to the multicultural nature of the East End community, bringing authors who have explored their cultures, identities and outlooks into contact with audiences who might want to see themselves in books. But this isn't just a matter of catering for people in our different corners — though there's nothing wrong with cherishing difference. With Newham Bookshop it's also about meeting and sharing. We live and work in a diverse society. The bookshop shows how we can also share cultures with each other, listen to each other, learn from each other.

Disadvantage: the bookshop has never accepted the equation, lack of money equals lack of interest in books. However, for whatever reasons there is a link in society between disadvantage and levels of literacy and we know that a disinclination to read widely and often is a disadvantage for people navigating their way through society. By bringing writers to readers in schools, libraries, community centres and many different public spaces, the bookshop has done all it can to break that link between disadvantage and lack of interest in reading.

The combination of what it does in these two fields — diversity and disadvantage — gives the bookshop an emancipatory role. Emancipation is a matter of achieving freedoms. If people are constrained by marginalisation and oppression, then society is failing in its claims to be universal and fair. No one can tackle this on their own. No single institution can tackle it on their own. What Newham Bookshop shows though is how one institution can give it a real good go. They help all who come into contact with them — writers and readers — to emancipate themselves from the constraints put upon us. This makes it a hopeful, progressive, enlightening place to be around.

A brief introduction

Barking Road stretches across the London Borough of Newham, snaking up from Canning Town. Halfway along this busy thoroughfare is Newham Bookshop, established in 1978. Inside you find a children's section hung with vines, a collection of adult books broad and diverse enough to suit almost any reader, and staff that try to find your perfect read with a few well-directed questions. And as important as its bookselling is its work nurturing Newham's readers and writers, organising events in its premises and further afield, bringing writers into schools and championing local authors.

The bookshop grew from local community action in the early 1970s, when Newham was short of school places and a group of parents got together to tackle the issue head on. They called themselves Newham Education Concern or NEC because they were sticking their 'necs' out. They fiercely challenged the orthodoxy that parents in Newham had low expectations for their children.

By 1975 NEC had opened the first Newham Parents' Centre in an old eel and pie shop in Prince Regent's Lane. In 1978 the centre moved to Barking Road and began to sell educational materials and books to families, in recognition of how difficult it was to access these things in the area at the time. This was how the bookshop began. Current manager Vivian Archer joined ten years later. Newham Parents' Centre expanded over the next twenty years to run twelve services, focusing on under-fives, reading support and career guidance. Once the Centre closed in the late 1990s the bookshop remained on Barking Road.

By 2018 Newham Bookshop was forty years old and had become a local institution, still not-for-profit and strong in the face of competition from corporate and online booksellers. When issues with the lease forced the bookshop to move premises two doors down the road, thousands of pounds were donated to finance the move and teams of volunteers spent days sorting through books and restocking the shelves.

Starting in 2019, Tania Aubeelack and I began recording interviews as part of the *Writing and Reading Newham* project run by On the Record, an oral history organisation. Guided by the bookshop we spoke to its staff, customers, collaborators and local authors. We asked the people we interviewed to tell us what the bookshop meant to them and to describe the role reading, writing and books has played in their lives.

The narratives in this book have been edited from a collection of thirty oral history interviews, which can be accessed in full at Bishopsgate Institute. The extracts chosen showcase the area's rich literary culture by including the voices of local authors, keen readers, library staff, parents, teachers, bookshop workers and volunteers, aged between 16 and 100. They convey what the bookshop means to them, and the place of reading and writing in their lives. They discuss the work of the bookshop in making reading accessible to all, the importance of finding books that speak to you and writers you can identify with; the need to value storytelling of all kinds; and the peculiar, imaginative 'spaces between' that reading and writing open in our lives.

Kay Zahmoul
Local resident and customer. She discovered the bookshop when she was six years old. As a parent who home-educates her daughters, she now visits the bookshop regularly for inspiration and supplies.

Next door to the bookshop used to be a chip shop. While we were waiting for the chips to fry, I'd just sort of look over. It was usually my older sisters that brought me out. I'd be holding their hand, and I'd want to pull away, to go inside and look, but they never let me.

One day I finally convinced my sister to let me go in. It just looked so inviting, especially the children's section. The way it was decorated, it always looked enchanted. There were some sparkly things in there, and there were leaves and trees, maybe there was a woodland theme from the latest book. I always wanted to come in and touch things. Eventually, we did come in and we were looking at all the books, and they were shiny, and when you opened them the illustrations were amazing. I was totally mesmerised.

And then it became a regular habit. We'd spend a lot of time looking at different books. We were more looking than buying, but Vivian always let us stay, because I always felt that she saw we were reading the books, and she liked that. Some shopkeepers might say, 'Come on, you're wasting my time. Get out, stop touching everything.' But she never said that to us. So, it became a place where we could come and just get away from the world for a bit, and get into a book.

Ada Varley
Volunteered in Newham Parents'
Centre and the bookshop for thirty
years, first as a literacy tutor and
then as a volunteer bookseller.
There is a plaque in the bookshop,
above the fiction section, which
was presented by Ada. It is in-
scribed 'for the joy of reading.'

I moved to London just before my sixtieth birthday. Before that I lived up north. It was just after I moved to the area that I passed the bookshop and saw a notice in the window asking for volunteers to teach literacy. That's when I became involved, I went in and volunteered. And that started quite a new period in my life.

I was born in Liverpool in 1919. This is my centenary year. My father was in the building trade. Work wasn't steady then. If there was no work you just got your cards and that was it. It wasn't a wealthy area.

We didn't have many books in the house. We had books for school prizes and things like that. But as soon as I could I joined the local library, and from then on I've been a member of libraries wherever I've been. So, when I couldn't afford to buy books I took them out on loan.

No one read with me as a child. We read at school, of course.

And eventually I won a scholarship to a grammar school as it was then. The teachers tended to concentrate on those with aptitude, so a lot of the other children were neglected. There were just two of us who passed the scholarship the year I did. So I went on to grammar school. And of course, they did encourage reading, and we had a very good English teacher.

I remember reading *Little Women* with my sister, who was slightly older than me. We used to read together and play act the parts. That was my favourite book. I bought it for my granddaughter many years later.

When I joined the Parents' Centre as a volunteer literacy tutor we were thrown in the deep end at first. We were just introduced to someone who needed help. But subsequently we were able to take City and Guilds certificates. I got one for teaching basic literacy and numeracy.

My first student worked for Remploy, which employ disabled people. And we never got very far with his reading skills, to be honest, but it developed into a sort of social thing, and he liked to tell me all his troubles as it were.

And then I had a local amateur footballer who had just been made player-manager. I was amazed by the fact that these men had got through all their school days but couldn't read or write and had managed to work. He had to make out the fixtures and allocate the players, so we concentrated on that. I learnt a bit about football, and he did make some progress.

I taught a young boy who had failed his O Levels a few times and he was desperate to pass. Looking back on it I think he would probably have been diagnosed as dyslexic now because he just couldn't spell. And we tried. He was very imaginative, he made up all these stories, and we wrote them down together. He was very keen on mystery and magic. He failed again, I'm sorry to say.

And another one was a young man who was taking a bricklaying course, for a builder's firm who promised a job if he passed. I learnt a lot about bricks and things. He visited me later with his hard hat on. He did get his job.

Later, when I retired, I became more involved in the bookshop. I was on the staff for a period. I stood in for someone who was on maternity leave. Then I was a Saturday volunteer. They had one member of the staff on Saturday, and us volunteers were on a rota to give them a lunch break. I was so handy nearby that sometimes I was called upon to do a bit extra.

It was very friendly. They had two cats at one time, which were very popular with the children. John Newman, who worked on the children's side, was very good at advising parents on what their children should be reading.

When my granddaughter was about five or six, she would come with me to the shop. She came on a Saturday lunchtime and made herself a badge with 'Helper' and her name on. She used to sort out the books and find ones people had asked for. She wanted to use the till, which wasn't allowed of course, and she was very interested in the shop cats.

I was certainly my own best customer sometimes. I always bought books. If you read a review Vivian would get it immediately, she was very good with that. And once or twice I sat in with her when she was interviewing a publisher's rep about what to buy for the shop. She always knew what would interest local people.

One day a customer came into the shop and enquired about a reading group, and so it was set up and Vivian advertised it. We had quite a few members to start with. There must have been about twelve of us, which is quite big for a reading group. It went on for about ten years. And of course we bought the books in the shop. We chose them by lucky dip; you put what you would like to discuss into a hat, one was chosen, and we read it. I think we met every three weeks. I made friends from the book club. I think my ninetieth birthday was the last one, because I remember them buying me this big cream cake.

It's a very community-based shop, the bookshop. Very community-minded. And a lifeline to me when I first came to Newham.

> *Mayuri Gajjar*
> *Local resident who worked in Newham Bookshop, as her sister had done before her. She remembers coming to the bookshop as a child.*

Coming to the bookshop, the first thing you hear is sirens. Don't freak yourself out, that's just east London. And then you walk into the bookshop and the first thing you see are vines everywhere, and the bunting, and the Roald Dahl posters.

You walk in. It's normally quite quiet because you just have people browsing. Apart from when the kids are here, then it's crazy. But it's nice because they are having a good time. It's wall-to-wall with books, the children's side is unbelievable. We recently had our new adult shop built. And in there everything's categorised, we've got a feminist section, fiction, nonfiction, self-help, biographies. It's all really beautiful.

Tom Williams
Has worked part-time in the book-shop since he was a teenager. He staffs the shop on Saturdays and is often to be found behind a book stall at one of the many events around London where Newham Bookshop sells books.

We moved in Christmas 2018, from number 747 Barking Road to 743. The old shop had become quite overrun with books. They had been there for years. It was very unusual, eccentric, and it looked a little bit like a second-hand book shop. It had a really wide stock and lots of unusual books that you couldn't find anywhere else. But maybe it wasn't brilliant for browsing because it was quite difficult to find certain things.

The children's shop sells a mixture of education books, picture books and story books. It's got a really nice diverse selection. It allows people with young children to get a good selection of books.

Then the shop for adults sells mainly three different kinds of books. First the practical books like dictionaries and course books for people training to be nurses and carers. We sell lots of books every week for people who are taking the Life in the UK test. Then also we sell some specialist nonfiction, particularly about the history of the East End and Newham, but we also have a lot on politics. And then we provide a curated selection of fiction for people in the area. There's probably not that many areas like Newham that have a bookshop with this selection of books. You tend to find bookshops like that in slightly more affluent or trendy areas.

Vivian Archer
Bookseller, former actor and the
manager of Newham Bookshop
since 1988. In 2018 she was
given an award for her outstand-
ing contribution to bookselling by
Books are My Bag.

I was born in 1948 in north London. My parents were both refugees from Germany. My father was an architect in Germany and they didn't recognise his qualification here, so he went into the rag trade. And my mother, she didn't really work all that much, but after my father died she did a bit of sewing and so on for people. My father died when I was very young.

As young children both my sister and I loved books. My mother had a very strong German accent, so we actually couldn't understand what she was reading to us half the time. We managed to learn to read quite quickly, so that we knew what the books were about and could read them ourselves. We were surrounded by, and just loved, books. We were brought up bilingually, so we did read some German books as well.

Both my sister and I loved classics. Absolutely loved Enid Blyton, read every *Malory Towers*, *St Clare's*. Just read everything really. We went to the library locally to borrow books.

But once a week we would be bought books, which was very special. My dad took us to a bookshop in Hampstead and we were always allowed to choose any book we wanted, one a week. And he was also a great reader.

I still love classics, Russian and French classics. To me they are still the best books around. And from the age of about 15 to 20 or whatever, I read literally every Russian classic I could get my hands on. *Anna Karenina* is still one of my favourite books. I love Zola. Things like *Nana* and *L'Assommoir* are books I could read and re-read all the time. They're wonderful.

Reading those stories gave me different worlds, how different people lived. And then of course, I did read a lot of modern books. I love women's writing, always have done. So, perhaps with modern books I read more women writers, who now are finding their own. Before, I read people like Margaret Drabble and so on, who were popular but not as popular as female writers are now. They're really amazing now, people like Bernardine Evaristo, Pat Barker, Elif Shafak.

Now I read when I go home and when I wake up early in the morning. I mean I'm reading less than I used to, interestingly enough. I'm not sure why. I only read two books a week.

But I also feel now that I'm not obliged to finish a book. I now feel, that if I don't like it, I will just put it down. I will give it a few chapters and that's it. And I never used to do that. I used to think, I must finish.

I became an actor after I left school. I had done my A Levels. Auditioned for drama school. I was very young, only sixteen, which they wouldn't allow now. But I got into the Central School of Speech and Drama, which I absolutely loved, and had three amazing years there.

I acted professionally for about ten years. The first job I did was with a big touring company. In those days, you had to do so many jobs a year or something before you got a full Equity card. But because of this tour, we went into the West End with *The Beggar's Opera* and I got my full Equity card on my first job. And then I did *Ivanhoe* and I played Rebecca in that. That was the first colour television series on Sunday afternoon, the first one in colour.

And then I decided that I would quit acting because I didn't want to be out of work, and I had the right look for the seventies. And so, I quit. And somebody asked me to help them in a little bookshop in Hackney called the Paperback Centre, owned by the Workers Revolutionary Party, which I had joined after 1968. A lot of actors joined the WRP actually, like Vanessa and Corin Redgrave.

Why did I join the WRP? I always had a very strong feeling

about what my family, particularly my mother more than my father, went through, having to leave Berlin. She lost her family in the camps. So, I mean that was always there. Though she never spoke about it. And I suppose that just made me feel very... Things needed to change. As I say, more now than ever.

And I loved working in the Paperback Centre. I think that combination of books and interacting with people is what I love doing. I got the bug. That's how I came to work in this shop. I was managing the Paperback Centre in Green Street. And then when that all fell apart there was a job going here. And I went for an interview with my daughter Rachel, who had literally just been born. I think she probably got the job.

That was thirty-one years ago. It was Newham Parents' Centre then. I mean it's completely changed from what it was. I believe that I was quite an influence on the changes. The shop didn't have such a broad selection of books then. I don't think there were as many people involved who read as much fiction and new fiction and so on. So I was able to bring that here.

There have always been ups and downs, there have been tough times, very tough times. You just had to reinvent yourself and work out ways of keeping going. We do stalls in parks, festivals, and that sort of thing. You've just got to go out, say 'Hi, we're here.' Go into schools, saying 'Can we bring you book stalls?' Getting authors in. I mean we've had some massive signings.

We had Benazir Bhutto in here. Just shortly before she was assassinated. We rang the anti-terrorist police, saying 'We're having her here; is it all right?' And they said 'Yes.' And it really was. My daughter was the main security. It was amazing, everybody brought their babies. So, she was here for absolutely ages. And then after she was assassinated they asked us to open a memorial book. We've still got people coming in saying 'We were there.'

When Hitler Stole Pink Rabbit by Judith Kerr was probably the book that meant most to my daughter, and still does, because it reflects our family. When Judith Kerr died I sent a Tweet out. I said that she came from the same background as my mother, the same part of Berlin as my mother, and they both had to flee, as refugees, escaping the Nazis. And that in memory of both of them I would donate a percentage of what we had taken in a week in the shop, which was more than I thought in the end. But I gave it to a refugee charity.

The principle at the heart of the shop is the community. Above everything, are the people we're here to sell books to, but also to talk to, and to interest in books. I mean, without a doubt, that's why the shop is here.

The future? Well to be honest, I should have retired some while ago. And I don't want to. I still love the hands-on. I must admit, I've probably enjoyed going to the events more than just sitting in the shop. Others can do that. You know, I love doing it. What can I say? But I'm not young. I'm still working very full-time. It's keeping me alert.

Andy Holland
A lifelong West Ham fan who

41

travels into London from the Midlands with his son to support his team and visit Newham Bookshop.

As a bibliophile the bookshop became an important stopping off point for me. It was probably more of a priority than going to the match sometimes, depending on where West Ham were in the league. It's just a cornucopia of the most amazing selection of books. You come here to expect the unexpected. I enjoy coming here to find that little gem, that book you hadn't thought about reading.

The concept on which this is run is quite important for me. It's a community bookshop and it's about communal exchange of ideas and views on writing and books in general. And it's non-profit making. And that's really refreshing I think, and it's against what is the norm in terms of the dissemination of culture. A lot of culture has become commodified but this is bucking the trend, and has done for some time. So, whenever I get the chance I'm here.

Pete May
Journalist, author and West Ham fan. Has written many books including Goodbye to Boleyn, *an account of the last days of the West Ham ground in Upton Park.*

I grew up supporting West Ham. Writing books about the club was a labour of love really. I've written quite a bit about my childhood going to football matches and that District Line journey from Upminster to Upton Park. There's a whole my-thology attached to that train line for me. It's sort of strangely romantic, for a kid from Brentwood, Essex, to be coming into slightly edgy east London, back in the days of skinheads and hippies in the 1970s. I remember getting on at Upminster, then the slow excitement, going through Hornchurch, all the way to Barking. And getting off at the station. I remember that because you'd see the 'Alight here for West Ham United' sign on the Tube signs. Going up the stairs, buying a programme, that sort of hubbub. Seeing all the people at the chip shop and outside The Queens pub. And quite a lot of memories of watching the last days of Bobby Moore and Geoff Hurst and those famous days in the seventies and late sixties.

So many fans would come into the bookshop before the games. I liked that you'd get people coming in for football books but there'd also be sociology and philosophy and politics. Vivian would have so many different things on sale. You'd discover football fans would be buying quite intellectual books as well. The signings were always really good. I remember Danny Dyer signing here and a massive queue outside. Clyde Best, who was one of the first black players to play for West Ham, I came to see him. There were always events and signings before games.

There'd be that hubbub of excitement and fans coming and going. It was a social place, you'd come in and you'd meet people. I used to enjoy the Christmas parties and I remember Vivian would have people like Benjamin Zephaniah, the poet, and Cass Pennant, who was writing about the hooligan days of West Ham, and Gilda O'Neill, who used to write about the old East End. So, you'd get this real eclectic mix of people at the events.

It's difficult to say what the impact of West Ham moving is, not living here. I guess all the trades have suffered. It's great to see Newham Bookshop still going but quite a few of these old institutions have gone. You can't fight change but it is sad to see the effect it's had.

Deborah Peck
Works for Newham Libraries. She had her first job in a small library across the road from Newham Bookshop at the age of 16. She is now often found organising activities and events in schools and libraries up and down the borough, sometimes dressed up as a character from children's literature. She occasionally takes a break in Newham Bookshop with a cup of tea.

I have a feeling of comfort when I walk in and there are books all lined up on the shelves. Even if it's chaotic and they're all over the floor. It's not about things being sparse, it's about them being full. Maybe it's the colours, maybe it's just the feeling that there are insights, wisdom, truths, imagination in here. The books cushion the sound. The warmth of the sound that's created with books is why you feel okay. It's kind of like being back in the womb, isn't it?

When I was growing up my mum read a lot and we had books in the house. But we didn't have stacks and stacks of them. And I never knew what to read. That followed me through to secondary school, when I met girls who knew exactly who they were as readers, and I remember feeling slightly uncomfortable about that. My friends were spoofing Georgette Heyer. And I thought 'Well, who even is this Georgette Heyer?' And laughing at Mills & Boon.

It was only later, going through my English degree, or finding the things that really spoke to me, that I was able to say, 'Oh, I kind of know who I am as a reader.' But I didn't know as a child. So consequently I didn't read as a child. And I think that happens to a lot of primary age children. If their parents aren't readers, if they don't have access, or if they don't know what to read, how do you know where to start? It makes me think of those shops that you go into where there's about four items hanging on a clothes rail and you go in and you feel really intimidated by the whole experience. That's how I felt about reading.

So, I think it's important to expose children to as much variety as you can and say, 'Well try this.' Or 'You like funny things? This is a funny author.' I think it exposes them to an area that they might feel uncomfortable with otherwise.

It's important children can feel connected to the books they read. I used to read some Enid Blyton, *The O'Sullivan Twins* and *Malory Towers* and things like that. I used to love the thought of midnight feasts. I had no idea what a lacrosse stick was. It sounded great but I certainly didn't find anything that was rooted in me at all. It might have helped, I might have discovered who I was as a reader a lot sooner had I found those books.

We've got a really nice group of authors in Newham, people like Irenosen Okojie, Salena Godden, Luan Goldie, Courttia Newland. When children meet authors at our events and see they are just a normal person, the world might open up to them. They might think, 'I could write,' or 'There are books out there that speak to me.' And I think that if we get a variety of authors then that helps children to see the possibilities of themselves as readers and writers.

A parent came into the Bookshop one day looking for books by a particular author for their child. They had been to an author event that we had organised at Stratford Library. The little boy had come home and he had been drawing the cartoons that the author had shown them how to draw all evening. And then he asked if he could go to bed early to read the book. The parents were so delighted by this that they came into Newham Bookshop looking for more books.

The books I read now? I always say that it's lonely women in cardigans that get me. If that's the central heroine then I'm going to fall for it hook, line and sinker. Like Elena Ferrante's Neapolitan novels. Because they are so intense and dark and they've got this relationship between two friends. I talked before about my friends at school and they seemed wildly intelligent, and I always felt slightly stupid around

46

them. Which is a little bit like the characters within the Elena Ferrante novels.

I read to relax and to take myself somewhere else. To go into myself and to be quiet, and just to connect with something that's just me at that moment. I read to be enclosed and to be at one with the characters in that story.

Andy Lane
Author of Young Adult fiction.
He grew up in the area not far
from the bookshop. He has written
many books, including the series
Young Sherlock Holmes *and*
Agent without Licence.

When I was growing up in East Ham there were a lot of libraries. I used to go to one and get as many books out as I was allowed, I think it was four books, and then go to another one and get another four books out of there and come home. Apart from WH Smith, which was the main purveyor of books when I was a kid, there was a market stall in East Ham Market where I used to go and hunt for second-hand books. But then a new bookshop opened just opposite Upton Park station, the Paperback Centre. And I thought, 'My God, this is brilliant, an entirely new bookshop.' And Newham Parents' Centre opened up on the Barking Road, which is about five minutes' walk from that bookshop, and I used to go in there as well and look for books. And it was great, because there were two bookshops and a library between the train station and my house. I was always late home because I'd pop into all these different places.

I have very fond memories of Newham Bookshop because they had the kind of books that you couldn't really find anywhere else, odd books, quirky books, interesting books. I got a book on burial customs around the world. Obscure little historical books, classics. It was like being in a library except you had to buy the books rather than borrow them. And I just had this obsession with odd little books.

At the moment I've become really interested in lost spaces and countries that used to exist but don't anymore. There's a beautiful book that's just come out, a collection of ancient maps that show islands that aren't actually real but that navigators thought were real and drew them on the maps. But then, 200 years later, when somebody went to look for them the island just wasn't there, it was fictional.

Being a kid growing up in London, you'd be on the top deck of a bus and you'd look out of the window, and there'd be all these little corners that were growing wild. And you'd say, 'Who owns that?' Because there was never anybody there. There was a space behind my mum and dad's house, between the back of their house and the back of the house in the next street, which was just a thin strip of land, and there were two huge trees growing in it. But nobody knew who owned it. I just became strangely obsessed with this idea of spaces that nobody quite knows what they are or where they are. And there's something almost fantastical about that, the spaces between the spaces where we live.

Which makes me think of this area that we used to play on when we were kids, it's where the Newham Hospital is now.

Looking back, I suspect now that it was a bomb site from the Second World War because there was a massive great dip in the ground, and we used to ride our bikes down it. It was surrounded by rough waste ground. And as a kid that space could be anything you wanted it to be. It could be a spaceship, could be an alien world, it could be a castle, it could be the Wild West.

Seeing those spaces and playing in them made me think about the history. How did these places come to be? But also the more fantastical element, that there's an entire world parallel to ours that we never see. Maybe people come and do strange ceremonies there on Midsummer's Eve. So, it's the idea that there is slightly more to life than we can see upfront. The only thing I've ever written has been about that idea, that there's something behind what we know.

Irenosen Okojie
Author of experimental fiction.
Her books include Speak Gigan-tular, Butterfly Fish *and* Nudi-branch. *She has won numerous awards for her writing, includ-ing the Betty Trask award for* Butterfly Fish, *is a fellow and Vice Chair of the Royal Society of Literature and was awarded an MBE for Services to Literature in 2021. She went to school in Newham and would browse in Newham Bookshop while her*

49

mother shopped in Queens Mar-
ket. She now lives in Newham.

When I'm writing I tend to get up really early in the morning because I like that state where you're in between sleep and being awake. I feel that time is really conducive to producing the sort of surreal writing that I enjoy doing, it's almost a hallucinatory state to be in. I keep my stints really short, usually two hours maximum. I write maybe three to four days a week and then I have the rest of the week off, just so I can let ideas marinate. I like to come back to the page excited. I don't like to feel like I'm writing a dissertation and it's a chore. Because I think if it feels that way, it shows on the page, it shows in the writing. So, I'm very conscious of enjoying the actual process. That's the whole point. It almost feels meditative, writing at that time in the morning. It's that thing of the world still being asleep, it's just lovely to write when it feels like the world hasn't woken up yet. So, it's a bit of magic.

I was born in Nigeria, in Benin, and I spent the first eight years of my life living in Lagos, a very colourful, hectic life, a full household, with all sorts of characters as well as my family being there. So there was always lots going on. And then, when I was eight, my dad moved me to England, to go to a boarding school in Holt, Norfolk, which was a real culture shock.

It was an interesting mix. I think that duality has made for really good fodder for my writing, just in terms of my cultural identity and always being in between spaces. And feeling slightly other, so feeling other in Norfolk, and then feeling other in London as well, because I had this posh accent and kids in London were like, 'Where have you come from? Who are you?' And I think that I'm always trying to explore that feeling through my writing.

The first book I picked up at boarding school was Roald Dahl's *Fantastic Mr Fox*. It was just so hilarious and so dark and so funny. It had this wonderful wackiness to it. And I just loved his writing, I found it really accessible.

As I read more, I felt it was like having the keys to other worlds, that there was some kind of power to it. I could not understand why some of the other kids didn't get it. They thought it was really geeky but I thought what you got out of books was amazing because it just showed you what's possible, and it's this thing of capturing your imagination, and sparking your creativity.

I remember that when I would go and spend time with my grandmother in Benin, sometimes the electricity wouldn't work, and people would gather around the fire and tell stories. African fables, *Anansi the Spider*, magical stories. There was always a lesson at the heart of it. People often say about my writing, 'Oh it's magical realism, where did that come from? Did you develop that when you got here?'[1] And I think the seeds for my writing were sown as a kid through the stories about animals who could do all sorts of incredible things.

So, when I trace it right back, it's not a surprise that I write the way I write, because it's in my literary DNA so to speak.

1 While sometimes described by others as magical realism, Irenosen defines her writing as speculative fiction.

My writing is fantastical so that relates to oral storytelling in Nigeria. I think its humorous as well, you're looking at people in tragic situations, but we know that humour is often intrinsic within tragedy. I think Dahl did that very well.

Toni Morrison has been a huge influence on me. I love, love her writing. Very often when people talk about black writers it's about their social impact. And that is important but I think it's also important to acknowledge how great she was at her craft, what a fantastic writer she was. *Jazz* was the first novel of hers I picked up and it was very much like the genre of music in its kind of freewheeling style. I was blown away by that. I was like, 'Wow, you can do this in a book?'

I like to leave a lot of space for unexpected things to happen. For me, the writing is an investigative process. I might be curious about what it's like for a young woman who's just lost her mother, who's struggling with her mental health, what does that feel like? And I try to explore that on the page. I will research it, I'll talk to people who have gone through those experiences. But I will never know this is exactly what it's like, and this is exactly what it should look like, because it's different for different people. So, that process is fascinating to me.

I don't plan plot right to a tee, I find that quite restrictive. I will have a loose idea of a story in my head. Sometimes I'll know the beginning and I'll know the ending, but I might not know what happens in the middle. I think 'Oh God, I've got to fill this space up. How do I get from this part to this part to this part?'

I think speculative fiction is clever in a way because it's the thing of it being slightly other worldly. You're lulled into this false sense of comfort because you think, 'Oh wow, these fantastical things are happening.' And then you can marry that with narratives that are about real experiences as well, which I try to do in my stories so they're not just fantastical for the sake of being fantastical. There's always something within them that I'm trying to explore about what it feels to go through a particular experience. For example, 'Gunk', the opening story in my collection *Speak Gigantular*, is basically a mother's rant about her son's dwindling mental health. But also what it's like to be a black man in this country. And it's really uncompromising but also quite surreal. So, the reader is reading it and is slightly uncomfortable. But also, I think, facing the realities of what it can be like to inhabit that body, to be in that space, to be in the city and the kind of struggles that we go through.

Absolutely, writing is a form of activism. I really feel that I'm disrupting some of the predictable narratives that people expect women writers of colour to do. And I'm not saying that there's anything wrong with those narratives, they deserve space as well. But I also think that there's a reluctance sometimes to open up that space. So, I've been fearless and active, in terms of claiming that space and fighting for that space for myself. Even when people were unsure whether I should be in that space, I knew that that space was important. And I would look to other writers who I felt had done that too, to have that kind of encouragement and confidence to go forward.

I hope that down the line some young woman of colour is going to pick up my books and say, 'I can write about anything,' because the narratives I write are so eclectic. Everything from monks to a man in a chicken suit committing robberies that's like a modern-day take on Robin Hood, to a young woman who's a Grace Jones impersonator. They're really quirky stories, but that's because I'm a quirky person and have those interests. And I feel there should be more space for that. It's important to show all the different sorts of writing that there can be and that experimental writing is not just for white writers. Often white writers get celebrated for doing it but there have been black writers in that space. When Octavia Butler first started writing sci-fi I'm sure people said to her, 'What are you doing in this space? Who are you to be writing these kinds of narratives? People don't write black people into the future.' When I think about the work that I'm doing, I look to those writers to gain courage and know that it's possible.

I hope that what I'm doing is expanding ideas of what black narratives are, what they can look like, what the themes are, what the subject matters are, the different contexts that we can be in. And opening that up so that we know that we can be seen in those contexts. It's that thing of if you're not shown something, if it's not reflected to you, you don't believe it's possible.

Jools Walker
Author who grew up in Canning
Town. Her book, Back in the
Frame, *was published in May*
2019 by Little, Brown. We met

Jools when she came into Newham Bookshop on Independent Book-shop day in 2019 and found her book on their shelves.

My book is a memoir, which always feels like a strange thing to say at 36 years old! It's about the biggest love of my life, which is cycling, and how I rediscovered cycling as a 28-year-old.

I used to cycle a lot around Canning Town as a young girl, partly inspired by my older sister Michelle, who used to ride around on a BMX in the late seventies, early eighties, when BMXing blew up in the UK. A young black girl in East London on a BMX bike was quite a sight to see. She was an inspiration for me because she didn't care about some of the negative feedback that she used to get. Being told that it was a very boyish activity, that she should be riding a girl's bike. It was her attitude of not caring that really inspired me to want to be just like her.

Michelle gave up cycling when she hit her teens which is something that happens to a lot of women and young girls out there. I inherited that bike and it changed my life for the better. Unfortunately, history repeated itself. When I hit 18 years old I stopped cycling as well. It was the usual thing with young girls, it wasn't cool anymore, everyone is learning how to drive, you don't feel particularly safe on the road, cat calling, things like that. It was one of the biggest regrets I ever had, banishing that bike to the downstairs cupboard. Eventually it got binned. But at 28 years old the desire to get back on a bike really hit me. It had always been there to be honest. Through the cycle to work scheme I ended up getting the bike of my dreams, which was a Pashley Princess. It changed my life for ever.

My book came from a blog I have been doing for the last nine years now, called Velo City Girl. I started it up because I'm an eternal journal keeper and I like to chart everything that goes on in my life. I wasn't seeing anybody like myself in the cycling industry and it is really hard to feel you can be part of something if you can't see yourself represented in it. Knowing how that felt, I thought, maybe if I do it myself it might encourage other women and girls out there. So, there was the joy of writing about it but also the hope that I could spark the joy off in other black women and women of colour out there who felt like they wanted to do this.

Having something like Newham Bookshop in the area is incredible. My mother used to come into this bookshop, I've come into this bookshop. Seeing my book on the shelves in the bookshop in the area I've grown up in is a dream come true. Anyone from the area can come in here and find a book that speaks to them, that says something to their soul.

I still think of myself as that girl from a council estate in Canning Town, who was told by people that you are not going to become anything beyond where you are and where you grow up. As amazing as it might be to go online and see your book for sale, it doesn't beat the feeling of seeing it in your local bookshop, especially one that's been around since before you were born. It means the world to me and it means the world to this community to have something like that at the centre of it, like a heartbeat essentially. It feels like a heartbeat in the centre of Newham.

John Newman
Bookseller, social worker and
expert in children's literature.
He has been working in Newham
Bookshop since 1989.

I was born in 1957. My dad was a lorry driver and my mum worked in shops. I remember being in nursery school and being very reluctant to have a sleep in the afternoon, and I was smacked because I just wouldn't settle. And then I remember being taken aside by the teacher and a nursery assistant, and they started teaching me to read.

We lived on Burdett Estate in Tower Hamlets. Every week the mobile library used to come. It was so easy, I could take myself to the library. As time went by, I used to get books for my brother, books for my mum, books for my dad. Mum read crime, Dad read westerns. At my primary school they had a little library. By the time I was in the juniors, one of the ways I used to get extra books out was to be a library monitor and tidy up the library and what have you. So that was it. My reading was always really important.

Reading took me out of the council estate, got me into grammar school, got me into university. It changed my life. I think reading above all was the most important thing in terms of my social mobility. My ability to read, to memorise, and to enthuse about what I'd read.

57

My nan famously once said, 'That boy, he reads so much his head will explode.' Which I've never forgotten. Always used to make me laugh.

I'd become interested in children's books before I started working at the bookshop. My wife, Julie, became a nursery schoolteacher. I used to go and buy picture books for her and we developed this huge collection.

We were dedicated readers of books to our children. There's a picture of me reading *Peace at Last* to my son when he was five months old. And you can see in the sequence of pictures how he's following the story. There's a book called *Babies Need Books*. I fundamentally believe that.

After I had been in the bookshop a while, I was asked if I wanted to go on the children's booksellers' group for the Booksellers Association. I became the chair of that for about five years. That led to all kinds of things. I was on the World Book Day committee, I was on the Children's Laureate committee for about three years.

The early 2000s was a very exciting time to be involved in children's literature. There was an upsurge in children's bookselling generated by Harry Potter's success. There was so much being published. I started reviewing for various publications, doing children's book reviews for *Publishing News* when it existed. For the last ten years I've been reviewing books for the school library journal.

I did a talk on the need for diversity in children's books and the need for publishers and everyone in the industry to get behind promoting diversity. And I said that even if Newham Bookshop was in a less diverse area, we'd still sell the same stuff. We would want to represent diversity because it represents our values. We're always interested, engaged and curious about people, curious about what they want to read, where they've come from, their experiences.

When the Net Book Agreement finished, we knew that it would be a struggle because we wouldn't be able to compete with supermarkets and the chain bookshops.[2] They immediately started discounting and doing three for twos. So one of the ways we addressed that was to start doing events. I remember we would be approaching publishers and they'd say, 'Where's Newham?' And, 'Who are you?' And, 'What's Newham Bookshop?' And, 'How many people can you get to an event?'

We had a lot of support from Gilda O'Neill, who always did her launches at the shop, Michael Rosen and Benjamin Zephaniah. And then it went from strength to strength. We did focus an awful lot on bringing black writers to Newham. So Malorie Blackman, Bali Rai, Narinder Dhami. These were the people we started doing the children's events with. And then we started building a reputation.

2 The Net Book Agreement (NBA) between publishers and booksellers fixed the price books could be sold at. It came to an end in the mid-1990s as booksellers and publishers withdrew, and was ruled illegal in 1997. The demise of the NBA paved the way for large bookshop chains, supermarkets and eventually online retailers to discount books and adversely affected small independent shops.

It's got to the point now where publishers will get on the phone and say, 'Look, we need someone to do this launch or that launch.' I call it guerilla bookselling. We get to places under the big boys' noses sometimes.

I do see my role as being a reader first and foremost. Because you can't sell books unless you read. If you're a butcher, you've got to know how to cut up a piece of meat. To be a bookseller you've got to be a reader. There's no way around it.

The first thing I learnt about selling books is you need to know something about the person. If they're not there and someone's buying a present, you ask, 'Who's it for? How old are they? What do they like?' Then you find things that might fit that description.

You can't stop technology. But there's something we lose when we don't deal with someone at a bank or a library, when we're engaging with a machine and we're not communicating. There's something very worrying about that, about our ability to communicate with each other effectively. And for years the bookshop has been completely about social intercourse, having a conversation. Talking about books and celebrating books. You can't celebrate books with a machine.

I wouldn't say that I relied on librarians when I was a child to find the books I wanted to read but they were there if I needed them. And they put the books on the shelves that I read, they selected them, they were the ones that helped me to see life beyond being a lorry driver like my dad.

What we do is encourage reading, that goes without saying. But we also promote writing, through the literacy classes that we used to run, through linking up with schools and the poetry and writing competitions we've done. We've sold books of poetry that children have put together through their primary schools on and off over the years.

The more you read the better writer you'll be. I tell parents this all the time. Parents come in who are aspirational for their children and they buy workbooks for them. I say to them, 'Look, this is great, but if you really want your children to progress, encourage them to read. Go and join the library. The more they read the better they will be at coping with their schoolwork.' If I had a pound for every time I've said that to someone over the years, I'd have a nice little windfall in the bank.

To encourage children to read you have a conversation. 'So, what do you like to do? And what do you watch on TV? Do you play with Lego? Oh, we've got some Lego books. Do you like *Star Wars*? Oh, there's a *Star Wars* book. Batman? Oh, a Batman book.' There's always a way in. Michael Rosen says there's a book for every child, you just have to find it.

Barbara Mackenzie
Local resident, parent and cake-maker extraordinaire. When her daughters were young she came to the bookshop to buy books with the message 'girls can do anything.' She makes book-themed cakes for

When my daughter was in primary school a new Harry Potter book was coming out and Vivian was selling it at midnight so that you could buy it as soon as possible on the day that it was released. I thought that was ridiculous but my daughter and her friends were so excited. They dressed up, made their own Harry Potter costumes and they queued up. We've still got the book and the carrier bag they came in. It was a really big event for them all.

Rachel Archer
Teacher, writer and performer.
Daughter of Vivian Archer, she
has been involved in the bookshop
almost her entire life.

I was pretty much raised in the bookshop, with cats called Daisy and Gertie. Books and cats have been a feature of my life. I would come in the bookshop all the time as a child.

It took me ages to learn how to read. Some of my friends were reading before me and I was obviously always completely surrounded by books. I was desperate to be able to read. I can't remember much about the early books I read, I think I was just so happy I was finally reading.

Now that I've become a teacher myself, I think the problems we have getting young people to read are the same problems we've always had. The kids that like reading still like reading.

But for some young people, reading is boring. 'There's nothing I want to read.' And I bet that's the same thing people thought fifty years ago. I don't think the challenges that we confront making society more literate are any different because of social media. I honestly don't. I don't think kids are more distracted. Everybody finds distractions if they don't want to do something

As I say to my students though, it's a bit like finding something nice to eat. If I didn't like carrots, I wouldn't just sit and eat carrots, would I? So, if the book that I've had in front of me for six weeks because school says I have to have a book with me at all times is not doing it for me, that book's wrong. But there are billions of books in the world.

I was in a lesson and there was some shuffling going around, something happening. I said 'What's going on?' And they were passing this Juno Dawson book from one to each other. It was about somebody coming out of a rehab facility. It's exactly what you want at fifteen. It's well written and she's a well-respected young adult fiction writer. I thought that was brilliant, that they were passing that around as though it was wrong.

I love Bali Rai's books, he's another really skilled young adult fiction writer. His writing is salacious, it's fantastic. And dark, which teenage girls love. I had given a copy of his (Un)arranged Marriage to Year Ten, and then there was some commotion because everybody needed to read that book. The library didn't have it. Oh, it was a drama, everyone wanted to read it.

Bali Rai also wrote a book about football. It was kind of an easy read and a boy who I don't think I had ever seen read but loved football, could not stop reading this book. And I thought 'Oh my God, we need 500 more books like this, so this boy keeps reading.' There are moments like that which are proof that you can get anyone to read.

I don't think you need to see yourself reflected in literature to start reading. We've got a bit obsessed with that in the discussions around literature and TV. I'm not like Jane Eyre, but when I was sixteen I saw bits of myself in her. Not because she was a perfect representation of me, but there's bits of that story I could still really associate with.

I think maybe it's topic. I say to my students 'Actually, if what gets you going is a sports biography, or a celebrity autobiography, fine, if that's what is going to get you reading words on a page.' Because they're normally written by quite a good ghost writer, so the reader is getting a bit of interesting vocabulary and they're learning how a sentence is structured. The point is they're not reading weird stuff on the internet that's not been edited. And I think that's crucially important. In Benjamin Zephaniah's autobiography he talks a lot about self-publishing, why it's not that good, because he needed an editor. And I've written stuff that's not been properly punctuated and whacked it online. There's nothing wrong with that but it's not how you learn to be a better reader or writer.

Luan Goldie
Author and primary school
teacher, grew up in Hackney,

64

East London and now lives in Newham. She has published two novels, with a third, These Streets, *expected in 2022. She won the Costa Short Story Award 2017 for her story* Two Steak Bakes and Two Chelsea Buns. *Her first novel,* Nightingale Point, *was longlisted for the Women's Prize for Fiction. When we interviewed her she had just published her first novel.*

When I moved to East Ham, Newham Bookshop was one of the first places I went, for the children's books mainly because I have a daughter. I also love children's picture books so much. I have quite a big collection of them which I use in the school where I teach.

I was quite shy about introducing myself to the bookshop as a published author. I had already gone in the bookshop quite a lot and then I had won the Costa Short Story prize. Even people at my work didn't really know that it was something I was doing. It is kind of embarrassing, going into a bookshop and saying, 'Oh I'm a writer.' I'm so new. Even when I meet other writers, I still find telling them 'I'm a writer' quite odd. I hope I'll get used to it, and then I'll be able to say, 'Oh I'm a writer. I actually have a book out.' It's like saying, 'Oh I'm a singer,' or... I don't know. It just feels strange. Because even though I was writing all the time, I didn't feel like I was a writer. Because writers are those people whose books I was buying and reading. I'm still trying to get used to being on the other side of it.

This year, when my first novel was coming up to publication, Vivian was really excited about stocking the book. She just said, 'You're local, we're going to stock your book, going to push your book.' And then she said to me about having the launch there. And I had never even thought about it. Because I thought, 'No, I'm going to have the launch in Daunt Books in Marylebone,' because that's what you do, you want to make a big splash. And she said to me, 'But you're an east London writer, and this is where you're from. Why are you having it all the way in west London, in a bookshop where you never really go?' And then I thought about it, of course, she's right, I've got to do it in Newham. And that was lovely, and I'm so glad I did. Some people I know from my yoga group came, some mums I know in the area. And just having that support was brilliant. And I like that I have a book there, and people come up to me saying, 'I just bought your book off Vivian.' It's really nice. I just feel so well supported by her and by everyone in the bookshop. It's amazing having your book in all the big bookshop chains but it's also quite anonymous.

I remember writing when I was in secondary school. I had a typewriter and I'd write with a friend of mine. We'd come up with these outrageous stories sitting up in my room and I would be typing them. She would have the ideas and I would write it down. We'd even sort of staple the pages together.

When I was about sixteen I was really into magazines and I decided I wanted to be a journalist. For a lot of people that age, when you're into music and films, that seems like a dream job, being able to interview pop stars and write up interviews. So my degree at university was in print journalism. And I went that way for quite a long time before I came back to writing creatively, writing stories.

I was a journalist for seven years. I was not writing about pop stars, I was writing about online media. This was when social media was just starting to happen, so we were writing stories about Myspace, Bebo and all those kinds of companies. It was an exciting industry because it was new and there was a lot of money. I was going to lots of really nice parties, getting loads of freebies. That side of journalism is great. But writing these business articles wasn't really what I wanted to do. Then I went and retrained to become a primary school teacher. I'm in my tenth year now of primary school teaching.

Because I've always read a lot it doesn't really matter to me what setting I'm reading about, what country they're in, what class, what race. I'm interested in everybody's story really. But I think it did make a difference to me when I read Courttia Newland's books for the first time. His early books are about groups of young people on council estates, and I was young, and I was on a council estate. It was just so familiar. So even though I wasn't really like those teenagers, they just seemed to me like people I knew. And I hadn't had that before.

And then Zadie Smith was the person who made me want to be a writer. *On Beauty* was the one that changed it for me. Just reading about the family in it, seeing the black parent and the white parent, the way the children were and just how familiar everything is. That book really made me want to be a writer, made me realise you can write stories like this about people like this. It's not niche, it's not only you that can understand it.

Working class writing shouldn't be so rare. But I do think publishing is trying to change. They're trying to open up to new voices. It's just quite late for them to be doing this now. But, you know, at least it's happening. It's a good change. Because we need more stories. Stories need to represent everybody across the UK, and we don't want these stereotypical stories either. Even when I started on my writing course, I was quite surprised by some of the comments I used to get on my writing. In *Nightingale Point* one of the characters is called Tristan. And I remember once being in a group where people were picking holes in that name and saying, 'You can't have a character called Tristan.' And I just didn't understand it because I went to school with boys called Tristan. But they were like, 'Well, it doesn't sound like the sort of name that a young black boy in a council estate would have.' And I was thinking, how would any of you know? Because they just weren't those sorts of people. A character in one of the flats at one point is drinking bottled water and someone had said, 'Well that's really unbelievable, why would someone buy bottled water if they were so poor?' And I was like, 'Well, it's not a poor character.' Because not everyone who lives on an estate is really so poor.

It's really strange. And that's why we need more stories like this so you can see that people aren't really that different. Sometimes we have a laugh about this in my writing group. The joke is always middle class people in north London having affairs. How many books are there about that? Like, we know everything about those sorts of characters. But then, a teenage black guy in a council estate? Maybe there are not that many stories about him, or maybe they're all certain kinds of stories.

I first started writing seriously when I moved to this house in East Ham. I had a baby, I was writing in her nap times. I think that was really good for me because I'm not precious about how I write. For me, if I've got the time, then I write. So I don't have any rituals or particular places. And people that do, I just think, 'Wow, you're really privileged.' Because, for me, it was just, 'Okay, I've got 40 minutes. I can write.' And I'd have my laptop switched on, ready for when she would fall asleep, so I could just hit the button and go. And I kept that habit up. When I have the time, I write. I'm not distracted, I'm not on the Internet, I'm not having a nap. I hear about other writers saying, 'Oh, just having a nap. How do you stop having a nap, or doing the housework?' I think, no. It's your writing time. It's so precious.

I don't go to cafés to write. I tried that in East Ham, it did not work. Because everyone in East Ham is way too interesting and distracting. I did try writing in the Costa Coffee and it was just a disaster. I actually wrote a whole chapter where two characters meet and they are in a Costa Coffee in East Ham. You know, someone is in there with their pack of croissants from the supermarket and people are going in to charge up their phone. I won the Costa Short Story Award and the managing director of Costa Coffee was there at the award ceremony. I just really wanted to tell him what the Costa in East Ham is like.

I meet my writing group most Thursdays at someone's house, sometimes it's three of us, sometimes it's seven. That group is so, so important for me. We edit each other's work. You bring a chapter, or even a synopsis, and you read it out. Then everyone sits with a copy of your work and goes through it, ticks, crosses, question marks. Because we know each other really well, we've been writing together for a long time, so we can be quite harsh on each other. Which is good because I definitely need that. There's no point giving your mum or your best friend your writing. They're going to love it. You need a group with other writers.

They've supported me when my book was on submission, getting an agent, getting a publisher, that kind of support has been incredible. Because it's been quite difficult at times and lots of people don't understand it. I was asked to rewrite my novel twice and it still wasn't published until much later. People who don't write, or people that don't do something creative on the side, it's quite difficult to talk to them about it. They'll just be like, 'Well why are you doing it? If it's causing you this much stress, then it's not a fun hobby.' But my writing group get it. So just for that sort of emotional support, they've been amazing.

If you want to write, you've just got to write. It sounds so simple doesn't it. But for years I was always like, 'Oh I want to write. I want to write. I've got all these ideas, I want to write.' But I was never sitting down and actually writing, just talking about it, thinking about it. You've just got to put in the hours. And it is hours and hours and hours. And it is sometimes tedious and frustrating. But you've just got to write. And you get better.

I love writing the first draft. I know it's going well when I don't know what time it is and I'm just completely lost in it. And the characters are coming to life. That's the best part for me. Then I can't write it fast enough.

David Ceen
Long term volunteer at Newham Bookshop. In 1980 he lived in Plaistow, discovered the Parents' Centre and got involved as a literacy tutor, later joining the management committee. Although he moved away from east London he remains dedicated to the bookshop.

In 2015 we had a World Book Day event at Waltham Forest Assembly Hall. We organised an event for 800 schoolchildren from across London, mostly Newham, Redbridge and Waltham Forest, but some came from Wandsworth and other places. And I did the seating plan. Because there were all these publishing types waving their arms about, and I thought, 'It's never going to work, unless people know where they're going to sit.' There were about six or eight authors who did performances and it was brilliant. All the children got free books, it was wonderful.

Dan Clapton
Formerly a TV producer, he changed career to sell beer at Wanstead Farmers' Market in 2013. He is now the proprietor of the

It was the start of the whole London craft beer movement. Every month I would have this visitor at my market stall and I used to say, 'Oh, that lady came back again.' She never bought anything, but she'd always stop and chat. She would kind of go, 'Oh, are you getting a venue?' And I'd be like, 'Yeah.' And she'd go, 'Oh, we do things, we do things.' And I'd go, 'Very good.' And I'd be really busy, and she'd always want to chat. And I used to think, 'Who is this woman?' And she'd say, 'Oh I've just done something with so-and-so, and so-and-so, and so-and-so.' And she'd drop all these wonderful names.

We kind of kept in touch and then I got this venue, the railway arch. And I knew that Vivian did events at other places so rather cheekily I said, 'Well, you could come here to the Tap. We've got everything we need.' And she went, 'Yes, yes, I've got an idea. I'll be in touch.' And then, about a week later she was in touch. And I just went, 'John Hegley, at the Tap?' I thought, that's amazing. And it sold out in about a week. To be fair I had never done anything like this. So, I was bluffing my way through it, saying, 'Oh yes, we know what to do, it'll be fine, it'll be fine.' And that sold out.

Where we are in Newham is a very interesting community. There's a lot of politically interested people, there's a lot of socially aware people. I realised we had this community around here that is fascinated by things. And I thought, if I can tap into that we can be financially viable by providing events that people like in the neighbourhood, without having to travel into London.

A typical event for us will be an author doing either an illustrated talk or being in conversation with another writer or journalist. In the old days, if we got thirty people here we used to think that's amazing, thirty people. Now, if we have less than fifty, it's like, 'Ooh, that's a bit disappointing.'

We had a night recently with the wonderful Esther Rutter, who is one of the country's leading authorities on the social history of yarn and wool, on a Friday night. How many people do you think came? About seventy-five. All loved it, from all over the country, all over London. They brought their knitting. Crocheting, they had to sit outside. But the knitters absolutely loved it.

Again, there's always a copy of the book for sale, drinks for sale. We try to keep the ticket price low and we make money on the bar, the bookshop make money on the book sales. We've had politics, music, social history, feminist history, knitting history.

People say, 'How do you attract people of such high standing?' And certainly we punch above our weight. That's all down to Newham Bookshop's pulling power. Vivian knows everyone and if she doesn't know someone they're not worth knowing. We've got Brett Anderson from Suede coming in December. I think the only other London show he's doing is the Festival

Hall, which has about 2,000 capacity. And us.

It is lovely that people have this kind of culture on their doorstep. Why should people have to go into London? Robert Elms was here a few months ago and he said, 'Culture comes from the dark and the damp.' Which is exactly what we are. We are dark, we are damp. We can't leave books here for too long because they go a little bit curly. People have this culture on their doorstep and it's here for them, like the bookshop is.

Karima Turay-Davis
Bookseller and reader. She lived
in Sierra Leone, Nigeria and
Ghana until she was 20, now she
lives in Newham. As a teenager
she discovered Newham Bookshop
on visits to London and when we
interviewed her in 2019 she was
working there part-time.

For people like us, who like reading, the bookshop means everything. It's our oasis, it's our place to keep our sanity. You meet like-minded people. It's such a vital thing to have.

I had an uncle who used to read poetry to me. He used to take me for walks, this was in Sierra Leone. I remember a particular hill, which is probably a tiny little hill, but at the time it seemed like the top of the world to me. He used to take me there and act out the poems. And, oh, they were just wonderful. He used to be every single character.

My mum used to read to me and give me books, and obviously growing up in West Africa I read lots of African literature. I was always quiet, not because I was shy; I was always finding ways to be left alone so I could read. I remember hiding under tables and just ignoring the panicked shouts of my family because I *had* to finish this chapter.

My mum did not approve of Enid Blyton. She thought that she was incredibly racist. She was very angry that I was reading these books on the African continent. But what child wouldn't like *The Famous Five*? The idea that you can go off together with your dog and have picnics. There was this girl called George, who I totally identified with, because the only time I was ever found in skirts was in school uniform, and I would scowl and hate it. And when we had deportment I was always being told that I should 'stop striding like a man, young lady.' So George was me, as far as I was concerned.

In West Africa we didn't really have children's books. We had a lot of oral stories, which I love, and I have passed them on to my son. My aunts and grandmother told them to me. My grandmother was Fulani, from a nomadic tribe. Some of her tribe settled in northern Nigeria, in Kano. I went to stay with her in Nigeria for a while, and she did not speak English at all. She spoke Arabic, Hausa, Yoruba and Krio and she refused to speak English. In fact, she refused to speak any of the colonial masters' languages. It was a point of resistance for her.

And what she would do was tell stories, stories that had been passed on. You would sit on the floor, and in Krio the story-teller will go, 'Ill!' And the people go, 'Ow!' Basically, it means

'You're ready for a story?' 'Yes.' [louder] 'Are you ready for a story?' 'Yes!' [louder] 'Are you ready for a story?' [shouting] 'Yeees!' then, '*Wan de ya*'. In Krio, that means 'Once upon a time', and the magic was off.

My favourite oral story? It was the king who went looking for his mother. He had everything in his life, except his mother. He did not know who she was and wanted to find out. So, he went on a pilgrimage. He knew one thing, and that was where he was born, what type of room and bed and so on. And so he walked from village to village, singing a particular song, asking, 'Who is my mother?' And all the different women came saying, 'I'm your mum, and this is the town you were born,' and so on. And they were all wrong. Anyway, he had got to the end of the world and he was totally desolate. And he thought, this is it, there is no way I will ever find out who my mother is. And there was this very dilapidated old hut with the rain falling through, and there was a really sad woman sitting outside. And he sang the song. And it was her. And she answered the question. That story is the one I always remember. My grandmother used it to say that it doesn't matter where you come from; it's the love that you have that will take you far.

Suresh Singh
Author of A Modest Living: Memoirs of a Cockney Sikh. *He was born in 1962 in Princelet Street, Spitalfields. In the 1970s he drummed in the punk band Spizzenergi. He became an architect and then a headteacher. When*

we interviewed him, Newham Bookshop was helping to promote his book. He now lives in Newham.

My book is a love story to my father. I thought that my dad had a story to tell and because he is no longer here, I had to tell it. Because a lot of these stories, they stay in people's houses, indoors. So I wanted to make it public and shout it from the rooftops. I think Paul Weller wrote a song about that once.

My mum and dad couldn't read or write when they came to this country and they stayed illiterate right to the end. But my dad believed that we should read and write. So they sent us to Sunday school and Whitechapel Library, which was amazing. They called it the ghetto university of the kids. And slowly I learnt to read and write.

It's difficult when you're bilingual. Because you're at home and you're speaking Punjabi, Urdu. And then you have to go to school. And, sometimes you don't understand the teachers. Because a lot of our teachers would not be from the East End. So one, they wouldn't have a cockney accent, they would be very posh. And you think 'Oh, they talk with a plum in their mouth.' I think what engaged me was pictures as well as text. Pictures of buildings and architecture. Whitechapel Library had a wonderful collection of art history upstairs. Oversize books. You could read a book on Degas and Matisse for free.

I think a lot of people think that reading and writing is all about text but I had this beautiful concept that you can read buildings and you can see text in shapes, in geometry and tessellation. I think that was a lot to do with going to UCL to study architecture at the Bartlett.

My father was a devout Sikh. To us the Guru Granth Sahib was the tenth guru that was left to us. And it's in the form of a book, in the Golden Temple, in all the gurdwaras. It's the book they stand in the middle. And what my dad loved about it was that Guru Nanak and the Sikh gurus wanted this text to be in Gurmukhi, not in Hindi, not in Parsi, not in Urdu. Gurmukhi was the colloquial language of that area. So everybody could have access to it.

I can't believe how my dad remembered it all off by heart. Everything was a narrative, it was told through storytelling. You make these pictures in your mind, and you say, 'Oh Dad, tell us that one, tell us that one.'

When my dad passed away, it hit me that I wanted to write a book about him and my mum, their stories. Because their story was unique, a Sikh family coming to Spitalfields. I think if you've got a story to tell, you've got to get it down somehow, please, everybody. Just write it down, and don't be so precious about it. And then get somebody to help you.

So I did it, I got somebody to help me, the Gentle Author. And then all these other people chipped in to edit it. I think it needed that. Because it's so emotional. It breaks your heart, some bits. Some bits I had to stop, and I said to the Gentle Author, 'I can't do it, this is doing my head in mate.' And there was a lot of crying, a lot of emotion. But he is very skilled. And you need someone to guide you.

78

As a devout Sikh, my dad had no connection to material objects. Can you imagine that? He would pick the fruit and veg up from the market floor. He spent all his time serving the poor. He said 'That's a modest living.' We can learn so much from that, from doing the best with what we've got. We don't need loads of stuff. Because he said, 'I ain't going to have you guys putting it in a black bag and put it in a skip. I'm going to do it first.' But he left these photos. And I thought, no one's going to put *them* in a black bag and put them in a skip.

I wanted the book to be in the library, and it's in the library, it's in Newham Library. And I did a talk at East Ham Library, and I'm so happy. My dad always said you don't attach yourself to nothing. You know? It's more how you talk to people, and what you leave behind. So the book is a legacy. People will read Joginder Singh's story, told by his son. And that's what I love about it. My nephews, young people, they go, 'Oh, *Cācā*, Uncle, we read your book, we read your book.'

I think he would cry if he saw the book. I think he would love it. He would love it's got pictures in it. And especially a picture of his mum. All the things that I think he would have loved, I put in.

The book has recipes in it because the food, the langar is so important to Sikhs. And the langar is one thing passed down to us, free food, twenty-four hours a day. And the sharing of food is so important. Any time, everybody who comes to us eats the same. And my dad wanted that always. If you come to our house you will eat exactly what we're going to eat. Dahl, roti, saags.

My dad loved crossing the boundaries. I had black mates, I had Jewish mates, I had Irish mates. And I had gay mates, you know. At that time, in the eighties, my mates were dying of AIDS. And my dad never ever judged my mates.

We were the first generation to be born in England. We were called blathees, the ones who are born in England. You go to India and then you miss baked beans and Tizer and stuff like that. Culturally you want to be in it but you're not. And then you come back here, and you're not in it either.

My dad came from the caste of the Untouchables, they were shoemakers. And they were the lowest of the castes. But in Sikhism, there's no caste. And Dad always wanted us to be able to read and write. I'm proud I went to a Russell Group university in the end. And I'm glad I went on to study architecture. I can honestly say, I can read buildings and I can read books. And that's really important to me. You know, not many people can read buildings.

Safiyah Saeed
Had a work experience placement in Newham Bookshop while she was at secondary school.

I read different genres. I mainly read mystery, crime, manga and dystopian stuff. My favourite author is Patrick Ness and my favourite book is his, *A Monster Calls*.

When I'm reading a book I go into a different world. When I come out I'm like, 'Wow.' Sometimes I read in my room but

I've got children in my house so it gets too loud, I can't focus, and I go out to read. Coming here to the bookshop you can purchase these books and read them over and over again and still get into a different world. You can read the same book over and over again and feel a variety of emotions.

Newham Bookshop has a wide range of young adult books, I still haven't read all of them. Last time I came I got a signed copy of a Patrick Ness book and I was very happy. I've kept it nice and clean. Let's just say I was bragging for at least a week. I still can't believe I have a signed copy.

Carel Buxton
Retired headteacher of a local
primary school. Has visited the
bookshop for over thirty years.

The bookshop is very much part of the community. It doesn't just sell books, it also sells information in a sense. You can come in here, ask lots of questions and get a lot of support. I've met quite a few famous authors here, including Benjamin Zephaniah, Michael Rosen, people with national reputations.

It brings people together who perhaps wouldn't normally meet each other and you make friends. It creates a sort of social cohesion in a way. In school you'd have an author visit that Vivian would organise, you'd sell the books, you'd buy a load for your school library and then the kids would drag their parents here in the holidays or on a Saturday. It is a centre of the community, in the way that a school is.

Newham is one of the poorest parts of the country so reading is always a priority for every teacher and headteacher in the borough. If you want children to be bookworms then making links with the local bookshop is one of the best ways to go about it.

It's so exciting for them to be read poetry like *Chocolate Cake* by Michael Rosen, or some of Benjamin Zephaniah's poems. They are very funny, the children love them, and suddenly the author is there. That is such a very meaningful experience. Recently, the *How to Tame Your Dragon* author, Cressida Cowell, came to a school in Upton Park and there were 600 children there. It was like a pop star was walking into the school. That really raises the profile of books and literature, and the pleasure children can get from the written word. And that's important because it is a lifelong investment. Once you've got a child that's a bookworm they can access all learning.

Vaseem Khan
Author of two successful crime
fiction series set in India; the
Baby Ganesh Agency *novels and*
the Malabar House *historical*
crime series set in 1950s Bombay.
He was born in Newham in 1973
and he grew up around Green
Street. As a child he would come
to Newham Bookshop on special
occasions to choose a book.

My dad was born on the subcontinent, as was my mum. They

came to the UK and I was born a year after they arrived. My dad was illiterate so books were not really on his agenda. My mum could read but she was busy raising kids. This dynamic is endemic to a lot of first-generation Asian families coming to the UK. But they worked hard and wanted their kids to get a good education. My dad was happy to spend money on textbooks, that sort of thing. But because money was tight, if I were to go to him and ask for fiction books, that wasn't really something that he could understand. The idea that I would want to spend money on stuff that people had made up didn't really compute with his way of thinking.

It was when I got to Elmhurst Primary School that a very friendly English teacher encouraged me and helped me to catch up. Once I caught the reading bug, I really got the bug. I think I was around nine when I discovered the library system and I managed to get my mother to take me every week. You could only get four library tickets at that stage and each week I would get four books. This was the first time in my life where I could choose the books that I wanted.

My mother had qualified as a teacher in Pakistan but she never really got the chance to teach much because she was married quite young and had kids. She was the one who spearheaded our education. We all eventually ended up at university, studying different things, and have had very good careers. In fact, two of my sisters are both secondary school teachers and that's largely been influenced by my mother.

Storytelling in the house was oral and it was a lot of stories about life in Pakistan. Infused with that were religious stories because my parents were Muslims and they were quite into their faith. They would tell us stories taken from the Koran, so you'd have stories about djinns, supernatural demons. These stories had moral lessons for us. We'd hear stories about a kid who supposedly did naughty things, and the djinns would come and get them.

My favourite book when I was young was *Danny the Champion of the World*, a Roald Dahl novel. Danny's father is a poacher. When his father is injured, Danny has to try and work out how to poach pheasants from the land of a particularly nasty local landowner. I think I loved it because here was this young boy who had to prevail against the odds. This was a down-to-earth story that could be real, it could be happening in any part of the country right now.

In my early teens I fell in love with science fiction. My earliest attempts at trying to write longer fiction were fantasy and sci-fi. I remember particularly that as a fourteen-year-old I came across the Terry Pratchett *Discworld* novels in my local library. Once I got into them I remember thinking 'Well this looks really easy.' Which of course it isn't, but Terry Pratchett made it *look* really easy.

I decided that I was going to write a fantasy novel as my first full-length novel. And I completed it at the age of seventeen. That was my first attempt to send something formally out to agents. It was absolutely awful. When you write something at the age of seventeen you neither have the skills or the life experience to be able to write a full-length novel and do it to the quality necessary to be published. But it was an incredible learning experience because the easiest thing in the world, as they say, is to start a novel, and the hardest thing is to finish one. That's why so many people who think they have a novel in them start off with great enthusiasm and then they hit a brick wall and their novel never gets finished. I spent the next twenty-three years writing six more novels, completing them all wherever I was working in the world, whether it was India or China, and sending them in to a bunch of agents. By the age of 40 I had collected well over 100 rejection letters.

When I was 17 my parents were unamused by the fact that I was wasting so much time on writing when I should have been concentrating on university applications. My dad particularly was not very happy that I seemed to be spending all my time trying to write this damn novel. They knew that this was a passion of mine but for them it was no different to my passion for cricket. It's a hobby. You're not supposed to waste your time on it because there's no such thing as an Asian person making a career as a writer, not in their experience anyway. What they wanted me to do was to go and get a proper job, be an accountant, be a lawyer, be a doctor. Be something that's going to take you a step further so you don't have to spend your whole life working in a factory as my dad did. I understand that sentiment but it cramps your horizons. It takes quite a strong will to be able to break out from that and say to parents, 'No, I am going to go to university, and I'm not going to study accounts, I'm going to study creative writing.'

Alas, I wasn't strong enough, I did do accounts and I ended up being a management consultant. But hopefully the world is changing, and more Asian parents will be willing to listen to their kids now, who say to them, 'I've no interest in being an accountant, lawyer or a doctor. I want to be in the creative arts, and I want to go and study it, and if it works, it works, but, if it doesn't, it's still my passion in life and that's what I want to pursue.'

After so many rejections, it was very hard for me to believe that anything great was going to come of my writing. That all changed after I finally got an agent and he sent my book out to publishers. He phoned me when I was in my office and he said, 'Vas, we've had an offer, not just for the book that you've written, *The Unexpected Inheritance of Inspector Chopra*, but Hodder would like you to write four books in the series.' I think I might have let out a yell in the office then. And that was when I got really excited because I wouldn't just be a one-book wonder, it would be a career.

I didn't write the first book in that series with any belief that it would be published. Instead, I said to myself, 'You're 40 now, why don't you write something that *you* really want to write about.' I realised that having just come back from living in India for ten years and knowing that I probably wouldn't go back to live there, what I really wanted to do was show this real India. And because I loved crime fiction, I thought, 'Okay, let's write a crime fiction novel set in India.' And then I thought, 'Well it's not going to get published anyway, so why don't I add an elephant into the mix.' The series is about a police inspector in his late forties, Inspector Chopra, who's forced into early retirement. As well as setting up a detective agency, he is looking after a one-year-old baby elephant. I don't expect people to take the elephant too seriously, it's more a metaphor for this amazing country that I found myself in. It allows me to add a bit of humour and charm in between Chopra going off and solving murders.

I'm a very organised person. My day job is managing research projects and academics, and so it would be wrong of me to insist that they stick to timelines if I couldn't do it myself. I come up with an idea for a story, usually a murder or something of that nature. And then I plan out who carried out the killing and why. Once I've got that in place, then I work backwards, and fill out suspects and red herrings. Finally, I decide on a theme, something I want to tell people about India that they may not know.

I usually spend three months writing a comprehensive plan of the book that I'm going to write. I mean really detailed, I use a spreadsheet, and I map out every scene with some notes. There might be sixty scenes in a completed novel. And it's only when I've got to that stage and done all my research that I will begin writing. And once I write, I write quite quickly. I'll write maybe 1,000 words every morning and it's about an 80,000-word novel, so three to four months of actual writing time after three months or four months of prep. It takes about eight to nine months to complete a first draft of a novel.

I write in complete silence at six in the morning, and the slightest noise will distract me. When I've got an interesting chapter or something that I'm really immersed in I become completely lost in that story, all of the characters become real. It's as if I'm having a real conversation with these characters. And I think that's when you know you're on the right track.

Because if you are immersed in a story, if these characters are as real to you as your friends, then that means that you are doing what a writer is supposed to be doing, which is to give the reader a direct pipeline into your imagination.

I now have a bunch of very close author friends and these are some of the guys I'm doing this fiction podcast with. The podcast is called the Red Hot Chilli Writers. It's called that because we are six British Asian writers, like me, who have grown up in this country. We aim to give a voice to people of our background breaking into the creative arts, have some witty, funny, intelligent dialogue and just let that infuse into people so that they get an understanding that it's no different me writing crime fiction as an Asian author, to a white person writing crime fiction. It's the quality of the product that should stand, the quality of the story that's being told.

Once my book was published, I discovered from my publicist at Hodder that Newham Bookshop and Vivian were held in incredibly high regard. They are one of the most famous and oldest independent bookshops in the country. And my publicist said, 'It's literally your borough. You should go and say hi to Viv.' Bearing in mind I had not been in for decades, I thought, 'What's the best way to do this?' I wrote to her and then I got a bunch of cupcakes and doughnuts. And I went into the shop one day and got chatting. And off the back of that we ended up collaborating on a number of events. Since then, we've been good friends and when Vivian puts on an event or something, I'll wander up. We did a big event together in central London where 700 people showed up and she sold out all of the stock she had brought along for the day. It helped that I brought in a couple of very famous crime author friends of mine. So the support works both ways.

When Newham Bookshop won Independent Bookshop of the Year, I was asked to present the award to Vivian. It was quite an emotional night for both of us I think. In the speech that I gave presenting the award, I said that it's probably quite rare for someone presenting an award like this to have been in the bookshop as a child, and then to have come back to the bookshop all those years later as a published author, and to have found a friend in the manager.

I ran a weekly book group in Manor Park Library. I was asked to do it by my younger sister, who used to work in the library system. She basically bullied me into doing it. But I'm very glad that she did because I discovered how much of a challenge it is for libraries in our country to try and combat vicious cuts to funding. Newham has been one of those areas which have invested in their libraries and they've tried to keep up staff numbers and stock. The group read one book a month and chose the books. We also chatted to each other. It was a sort of therapy as one of my book group readers said.

Let's think ahead. If as a society we do not invest, do not protect, do not support bookshops and libraries, then there will be a future, whether it's ten years or fifty years or one hundred years from now, when these things will disappear. And we have to ask ourselves, what kind of legacy, what kind of society do we want future generations to grow up in? Do we not want them to have easy access to books? Do we want all access to books to be controlled by just a couple of very large organisations? How egalitarian a society are we wanting to leave behind for future generations? And I think that Newham Bookshop, other bookshops, libraries, they're all part of that foundation, that structure, that we need to support.

Afterword

Tania Aubeelack worked with On the Record in 2019 after taking part in the youth-led project Fighting Sus! She became involved in all aspects of this project, helping to record many of the interviews in this book and she curated content for the learning resources for primary schools the project produced. She writes:

I will surely remember the interviews I did with customers visiting and browsing at Newham Bookshop. They each had a special and unique connection to reading. I will especially treasure the memory of a father saying that one of his proudest moments was when his daughter asked of her own accord if they could go to Newham Bookshop.

Before this project, I used to buy my books at mainstream corporate bookshops, but now I try to buy them at local bookshops. It was an eye-opener to have seen behind the scenes of a community bookshop like Newham Bookshop. It pays attention to the people it caters for and embodies values such as service, connection, diversity, accountability and safety.

I shall carry with me Vaseem Khan's determination and

passion for writing. Even after being rejected so many times, he did not let this taint his love for writing and it was when he least expected it that he got his book deal. I think that life has a way of making things work in the end.

95